CONTENTS

BORN STRONG

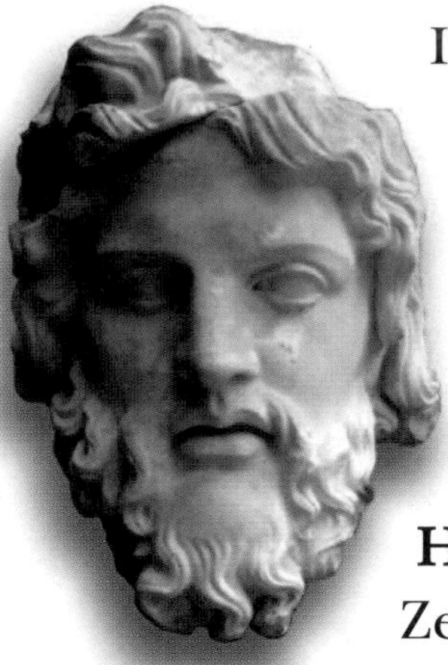

In Greek mythology, Hercules was the greatest hero of them all. He was the son of the god Zeus and Alcmene, a mortal woman, and was born in Tiryns, Mycene. Being the son of Zeus, Hercules was gifted with extraordinary natural strength.

As king of the gods, Zeus could do what he pleased, which drove his wife, Hera, crazy.

HERA'S GIFT

Zeus's wife, Hera, was very jealous and angry when Hercules was born. She sent snakes into his crib to kill him, but Hercules caught the snakes and strangled them—the first of his heroic deeds. Hera secretly vowed to keep on trying.

Hercules would grow up to be a brave and capable warrior, abilities that would stand him in good stead for the trials to come.

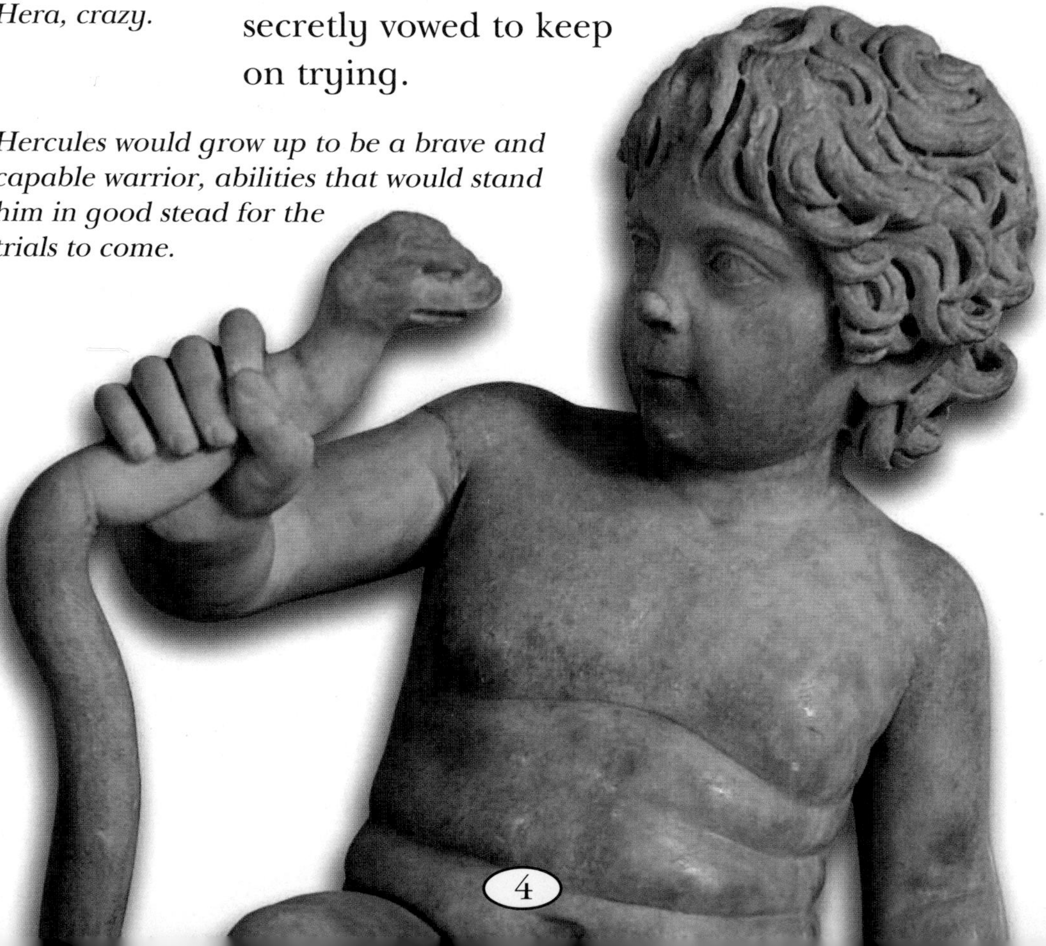

GRAPHIC MYTHICAL HEROES

HERCULES
FIGHTS THE NEMEAN LION

BY GARY JEFFREY
ILLUSTRATED BY TERRY RILEY

Gareth Stevens
Publishing

Please visit our website, www.garethstevens.com.
For a free color catalog of all our high-quality books,
call toll free 1-800-542-2595 or fax 1-877-542-2596.

Library of Congress Cataloging-in-Publication Data

Jeffrey, Gary.
Hercules fights the Nemean lion / Gary Jeffrey.
p. cm. — (Graphic mythical heroes)
Includes index.
ISBN 978-1-4339-7512-7 (pbk.)
ISBN 978-1-4339-7513-4 (6-pack)
ISBN 978-1-4339-7511-0 (library binding)
1. Hercules (Greek mythology)—Juvenile literature. 2. Nemean lion
(Greek mythology)—Juvenile literature. I. Title.
BL820.H5J44 2012
398.20938'02—dc23
2011050609

First Edition

Published in 2013 by
Gareth Stevens Publishing
111 East 14th Street, Suite 349
New York, NY 10003

Designed by David West Books

Photo credits:
p4, Sandstein; p5t, Foto Ad Meskens, p5b, Tetraktys

Printed in China

CPSIA compliance information: Batch #DWS12GS: For further information contact Gareth Stevens, New York, New York at 1-800-542-2595.

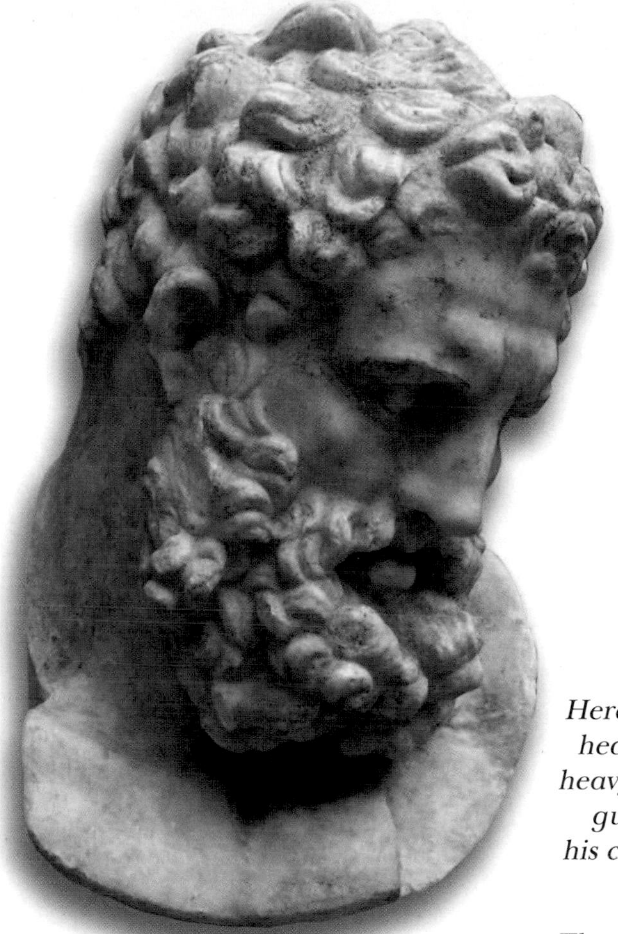

A Fit of Madness

Hercules married Megara, had children, and seemed intended for a happy life, when Hera put a spell of madness upon him.

In a fit of blind rage, he killed his wife and children. When he came to and realized what he had done, he went to the oracle of Delphi for help.

Hercules's heart lay heavy with guilt for his crimes.

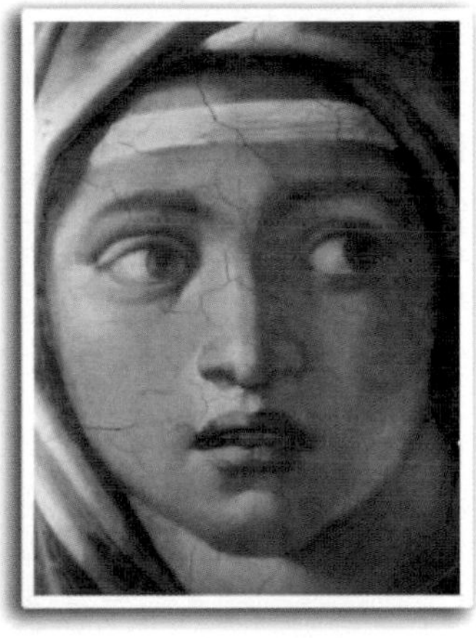

The oracle of Delphi was a priestess who had the powers of prophecy.

Ten Labors

The oracle told him he must perform ten tasks, or labors, to be set by his cousin Eurystheus, king of Mycene. Hercules understood that if he completed the labors to Eurystheus's satisfaction, his penance would be paid. The gods would take away his guilt and make him immortal...

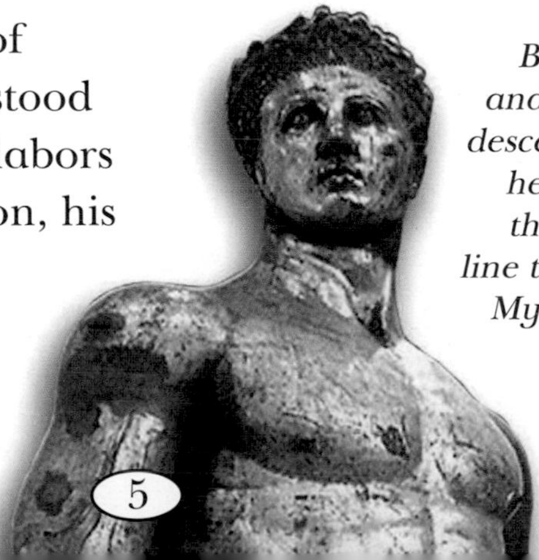

Both Eurystheus and Hercules were descended from the hero Perseus and therefore were in line to the throne of Mycene, but Hera made sure Eurystheus got it first.

Hercules Fights the Nemean Lion

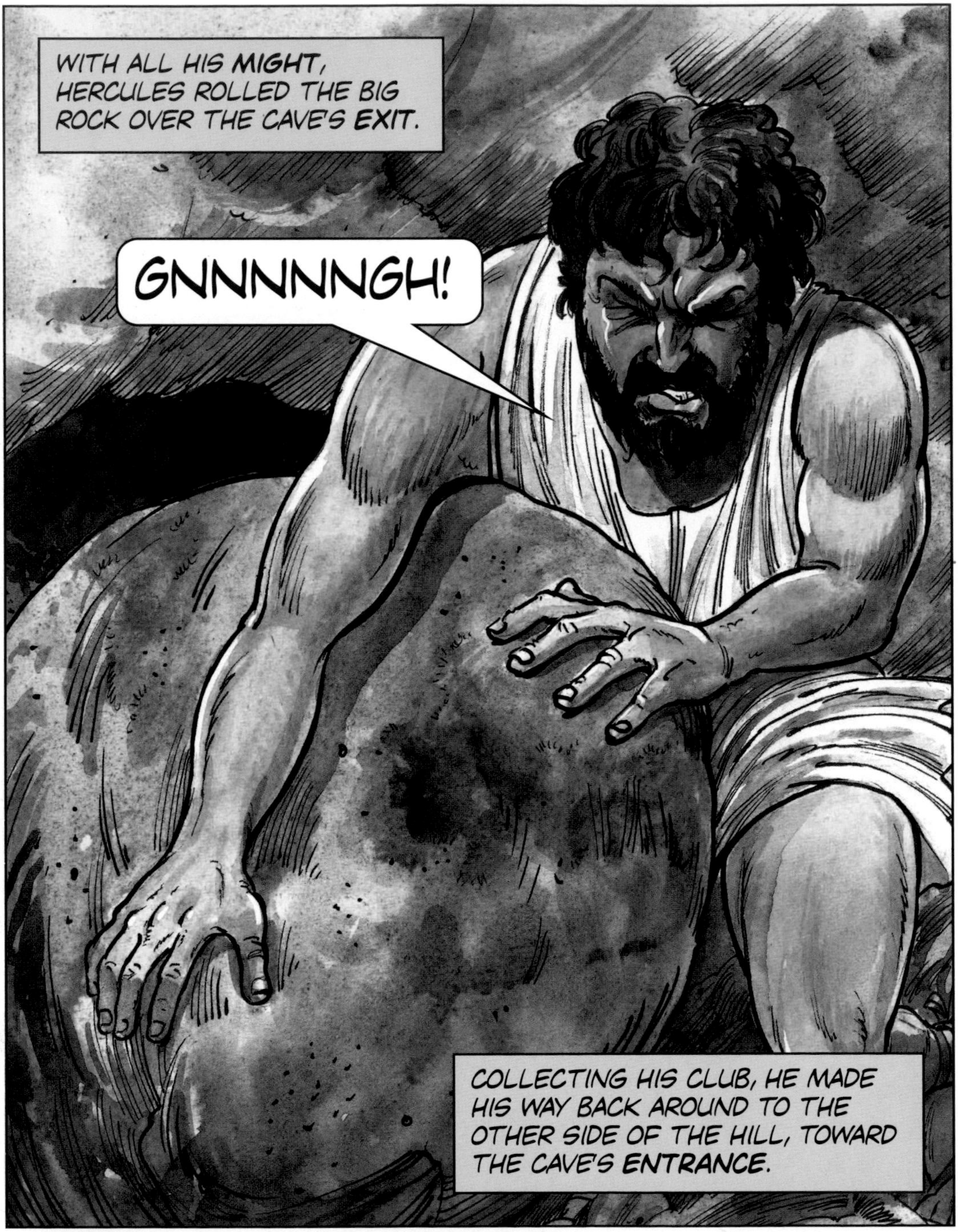
WITH ALL HIS MIGHT, HERCULES ROLLED THE BIG ROCK OVER THE CAVE'S EXIT.
GNNNNNGH!
COLLECTING HIS CLUB, HE MADE HIS WAY BACK AROUND TO THE OTHER SIDE OF THE HILL, TOWARD THE CAVE'S ENTRANCE.

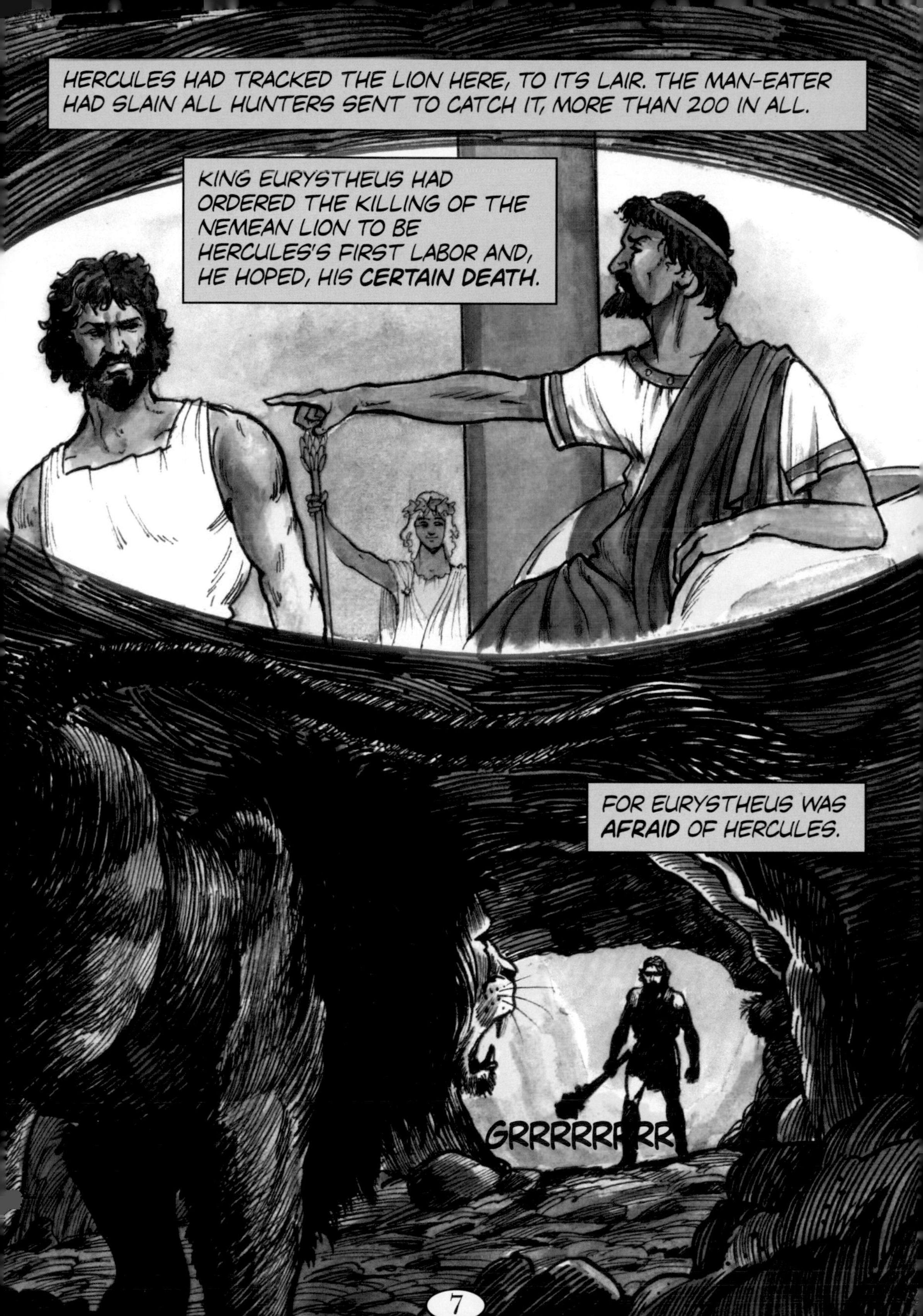
HERCULES HAD TRACKED THE LION HERE, TO ITS LAIR. THE MAN-EATER HAD SLAIN ALL HUNTERS SENT TO CATCH IT, MORE THAN 200 IN ALL.
KING EURYSTHEUS HAD ORDERED THE KILLING OF THE NEMEAN LION TO BE HERCULES'S FIRST LABOR AND, HE HOPED, HIS **CERTAIN DEATH.**
FOR EURYSTHEUS WAS **AFRAID** OF HERCULES.
GRRRRRRRR

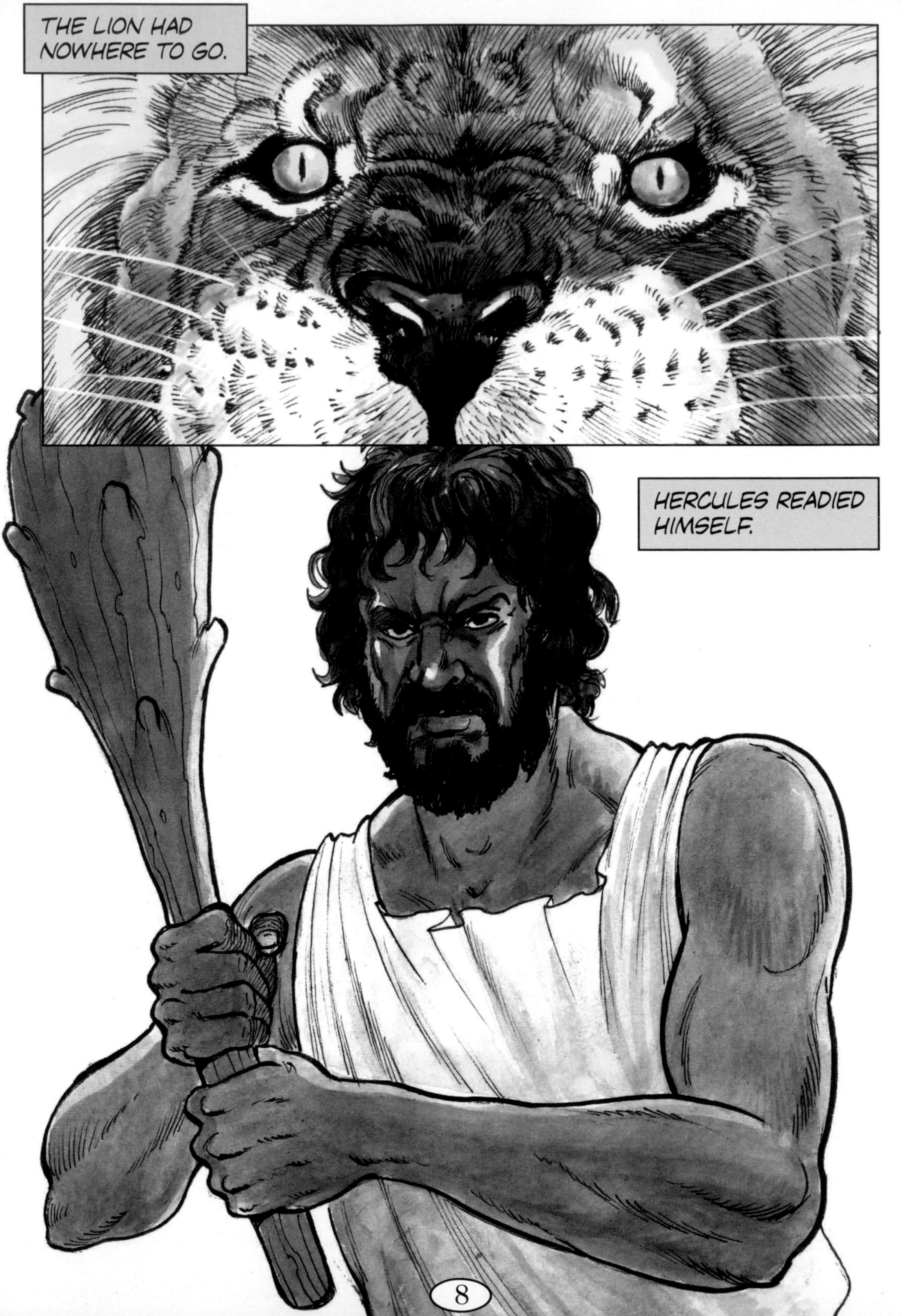
THE LION HAD NOWHERE TO GO.
HERCULES READIED HIMSELF.

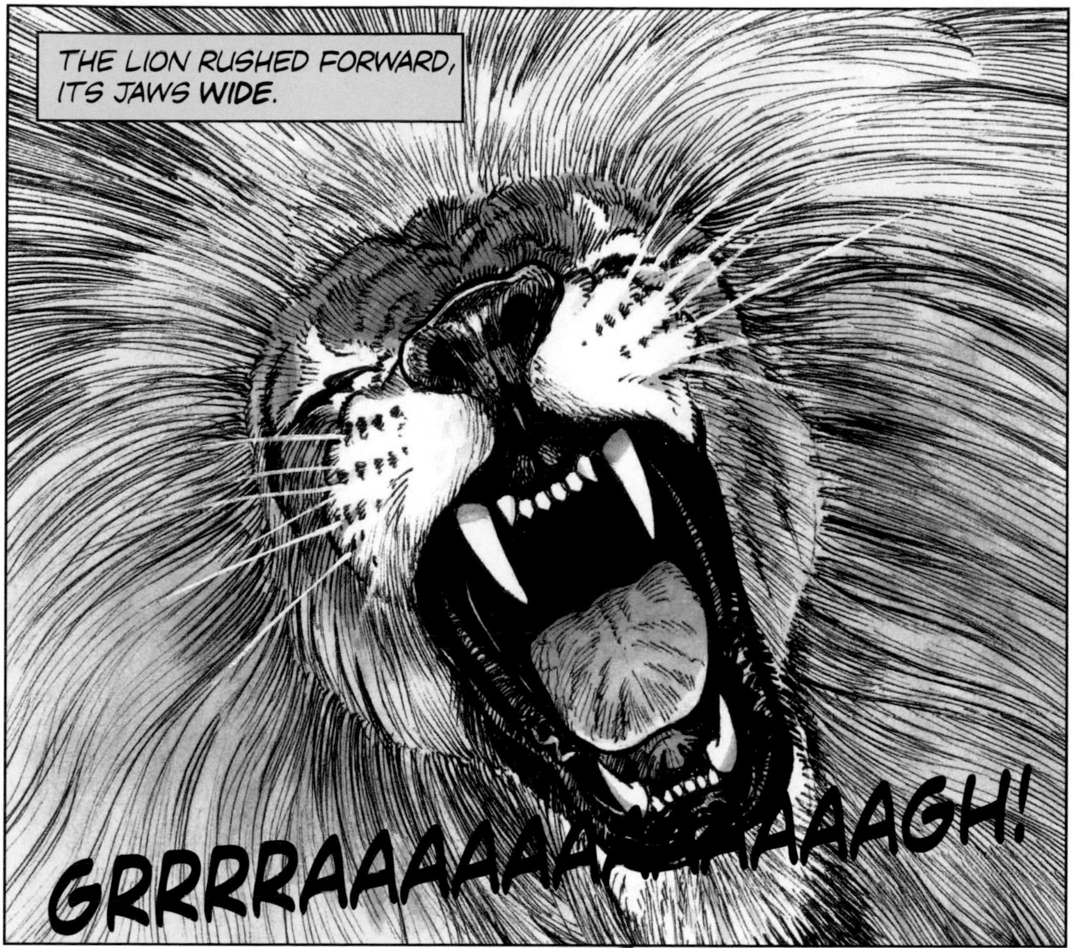
THE LION RUSHED FORWARD, ITS JAWS WIDE.
GRRRRAAAAAAAAAAAAAGH!

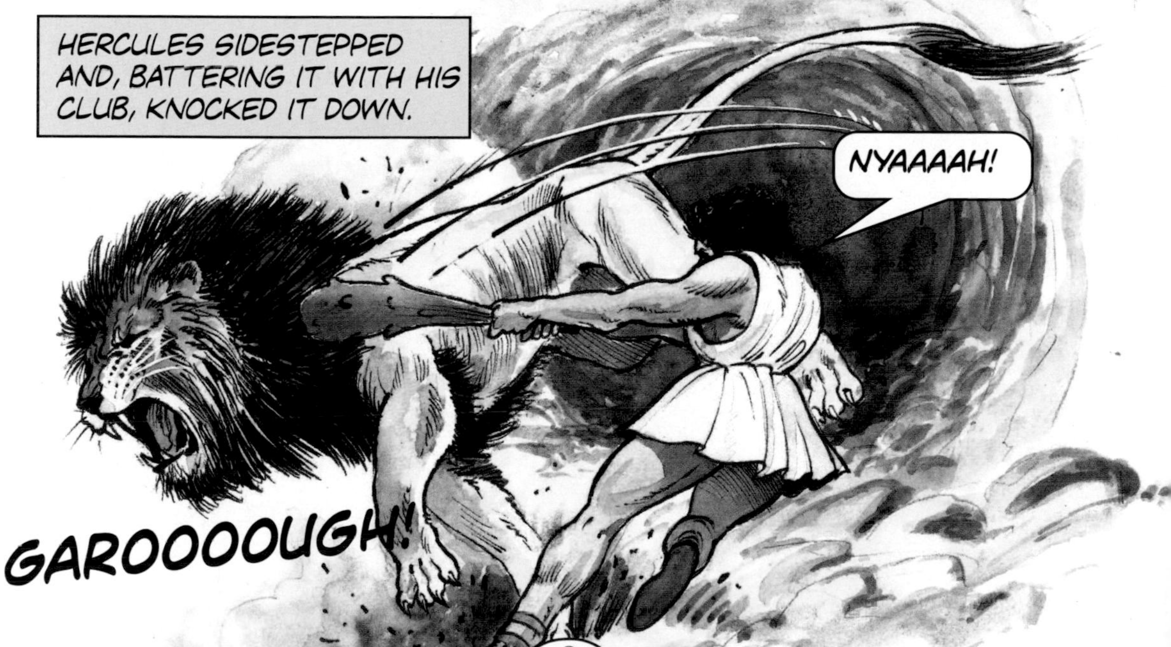
HERCULES SIDESTEPPED AND, BATTERING IT WITH HIS CLUB, KNOCKED IT DOWN.
NYAAAAH!
GAROOOOOUGH!

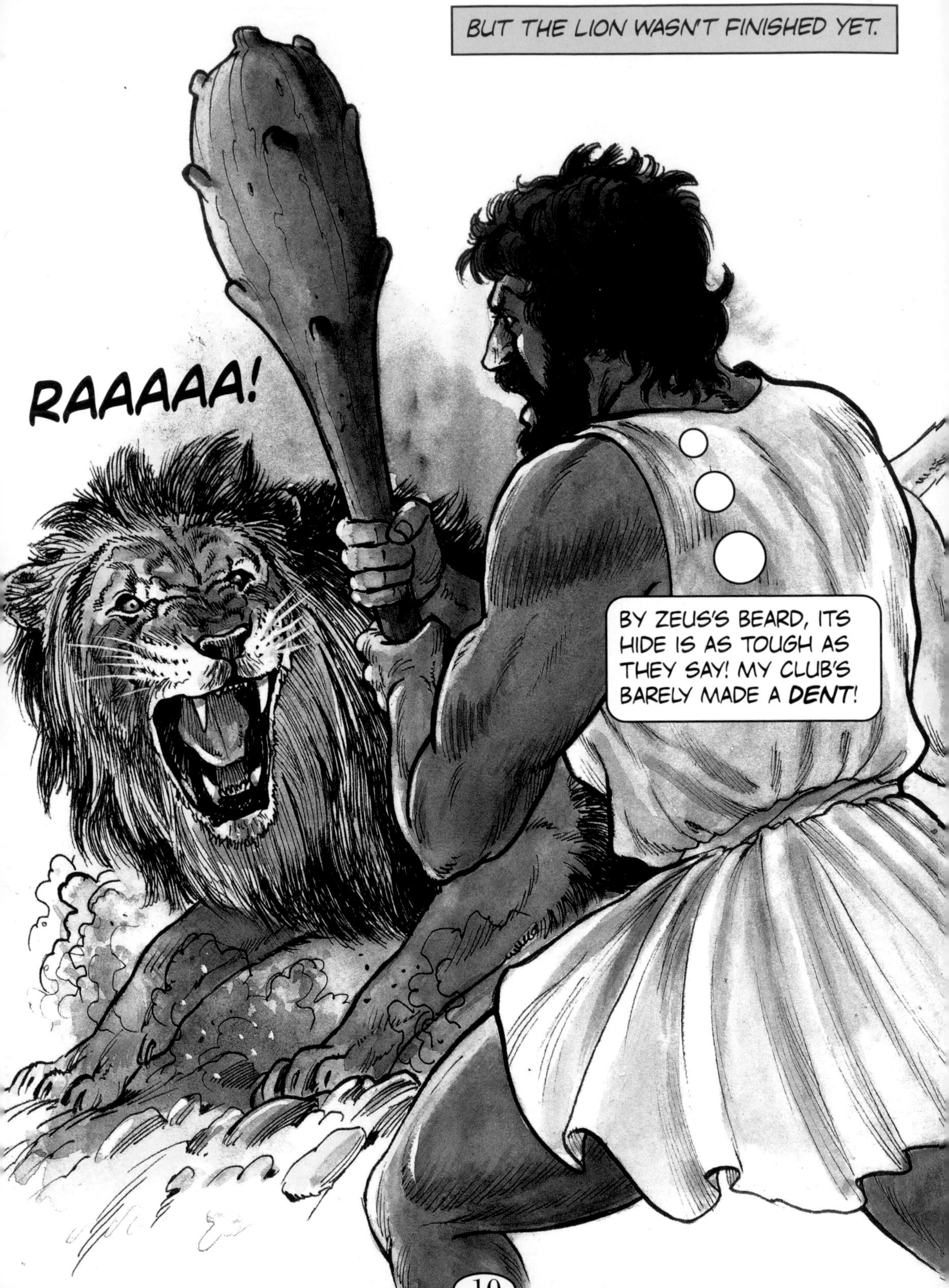
BUT THE LION WASN'T FINISHED YET.
RAAAAA!
BY ZEUS'S BEARD, ITS HIDE IS AS TOUGH AS THEY SAY! MY CLUB'S BARELY MADE A DENT!

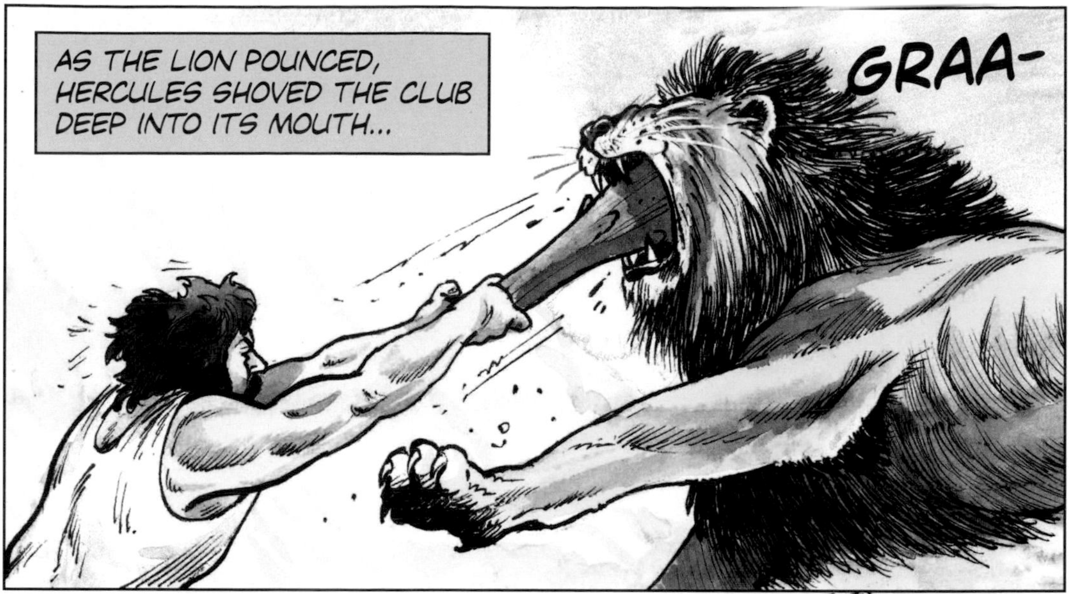
AS THE LION POUNCED, HERCULES SHOVED THE CLUB DEEP INTO ITS MOUTH...
GRAA-

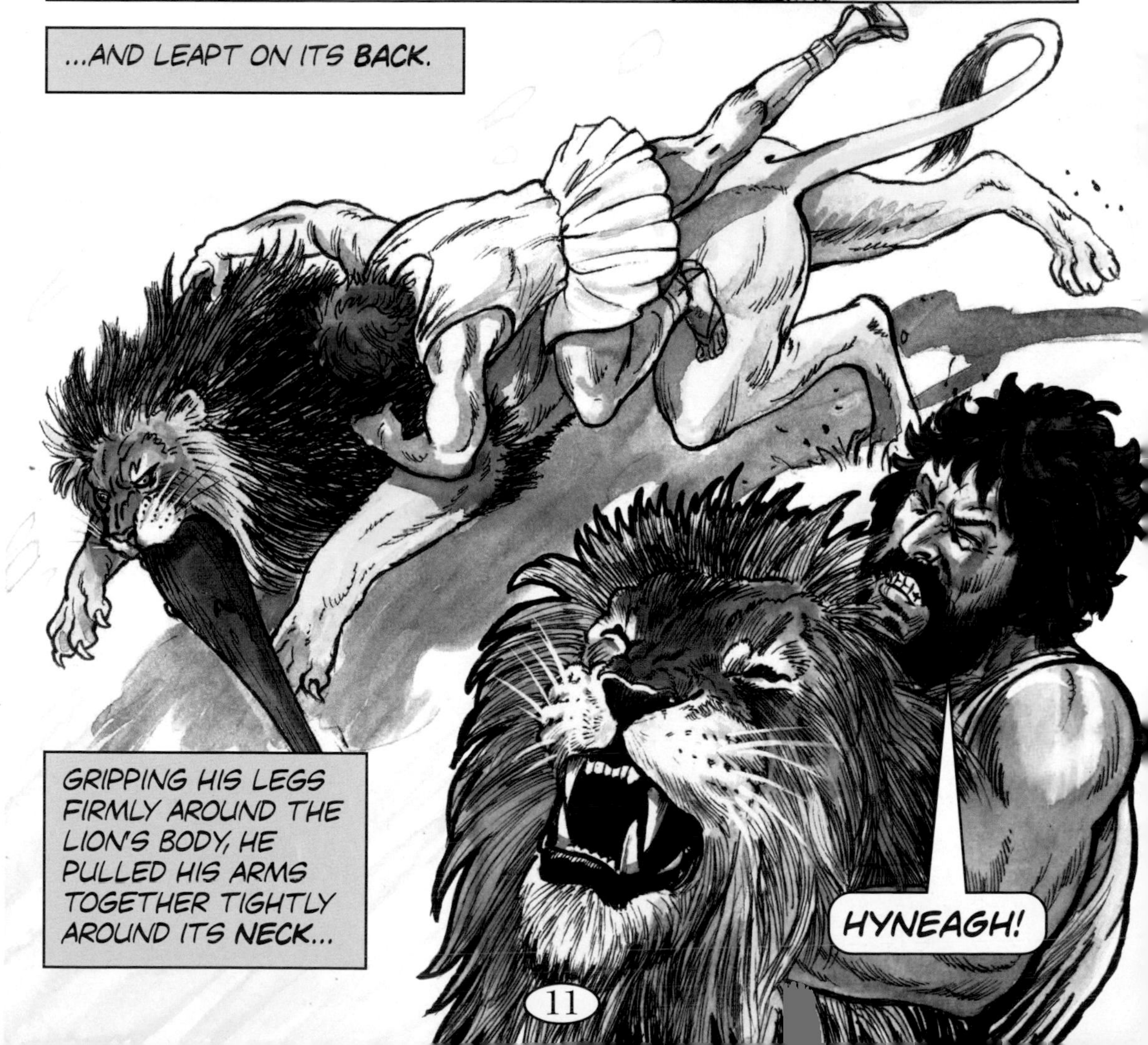
...AND LEAPT ON ITS BACK.
GRIPPING HIS LEGS FIRMLY AROUND THE LION'S BODY, HE PULLED HIS ARMS TOGETHER TIGHTLY AROUND ITS NECK...
HYNEAGH!

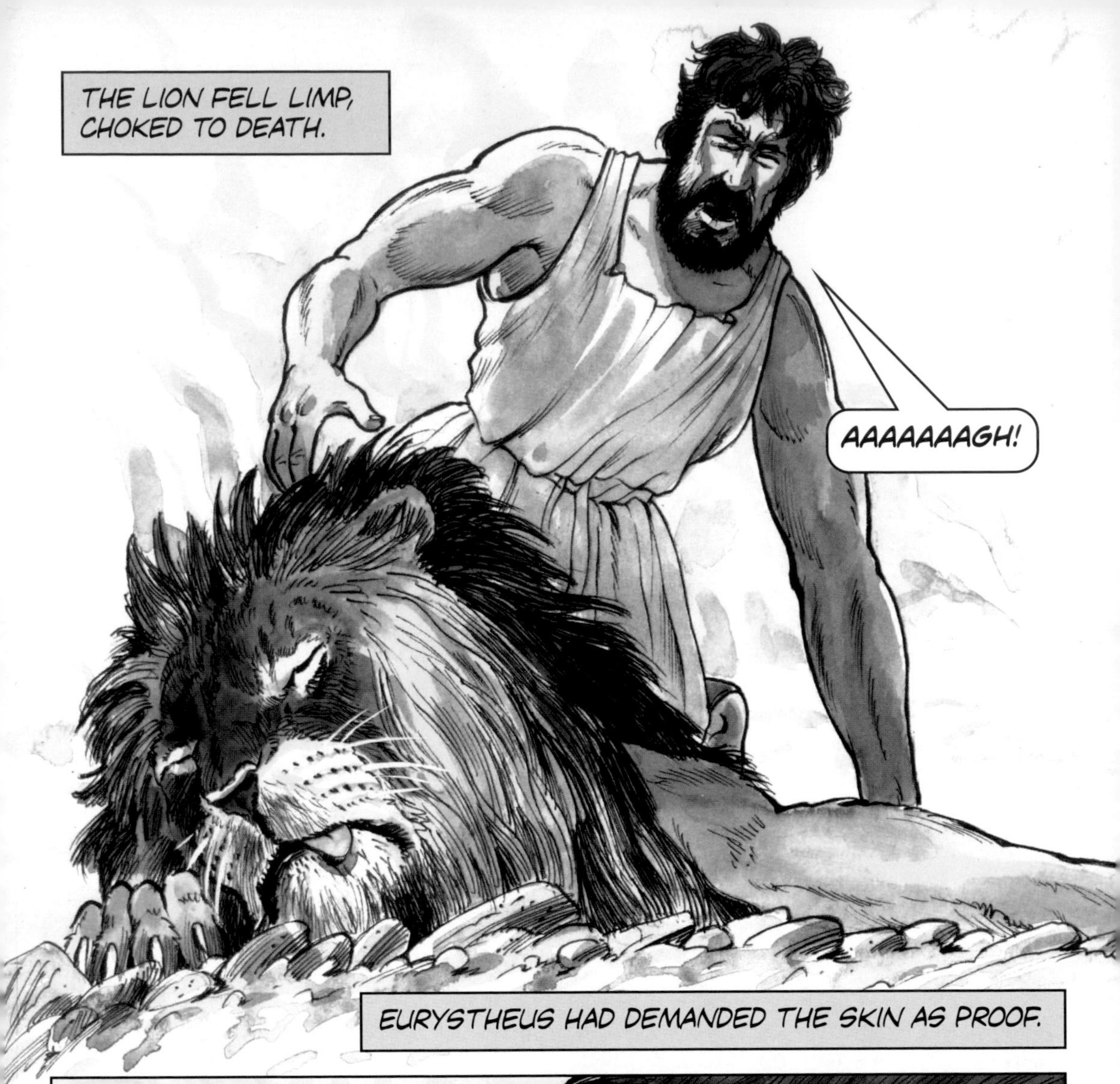
THE LION FELL LIMP, CHOKED TO DEATH.
AAAAAAAGH!
EURYSTHEUS HAD DEMANDED THE SKIN AS PROOF.

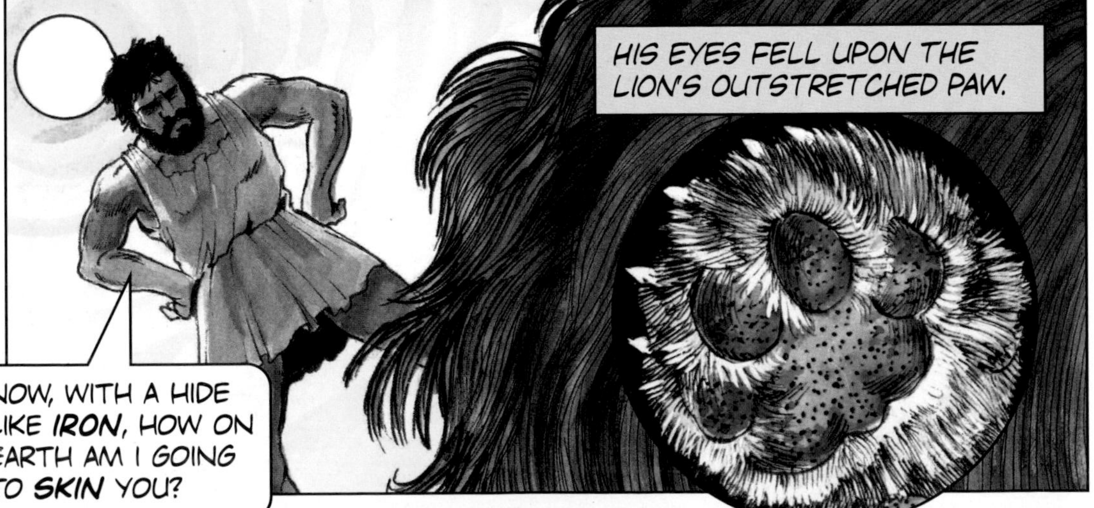
HIS EYES FELL UPON THE LION'S OUTSTRETCHED PAW.
NOW, WITH A HIDE LIKE IRON, HOW ON EARTH AM I GOING TO SKIN YOU?

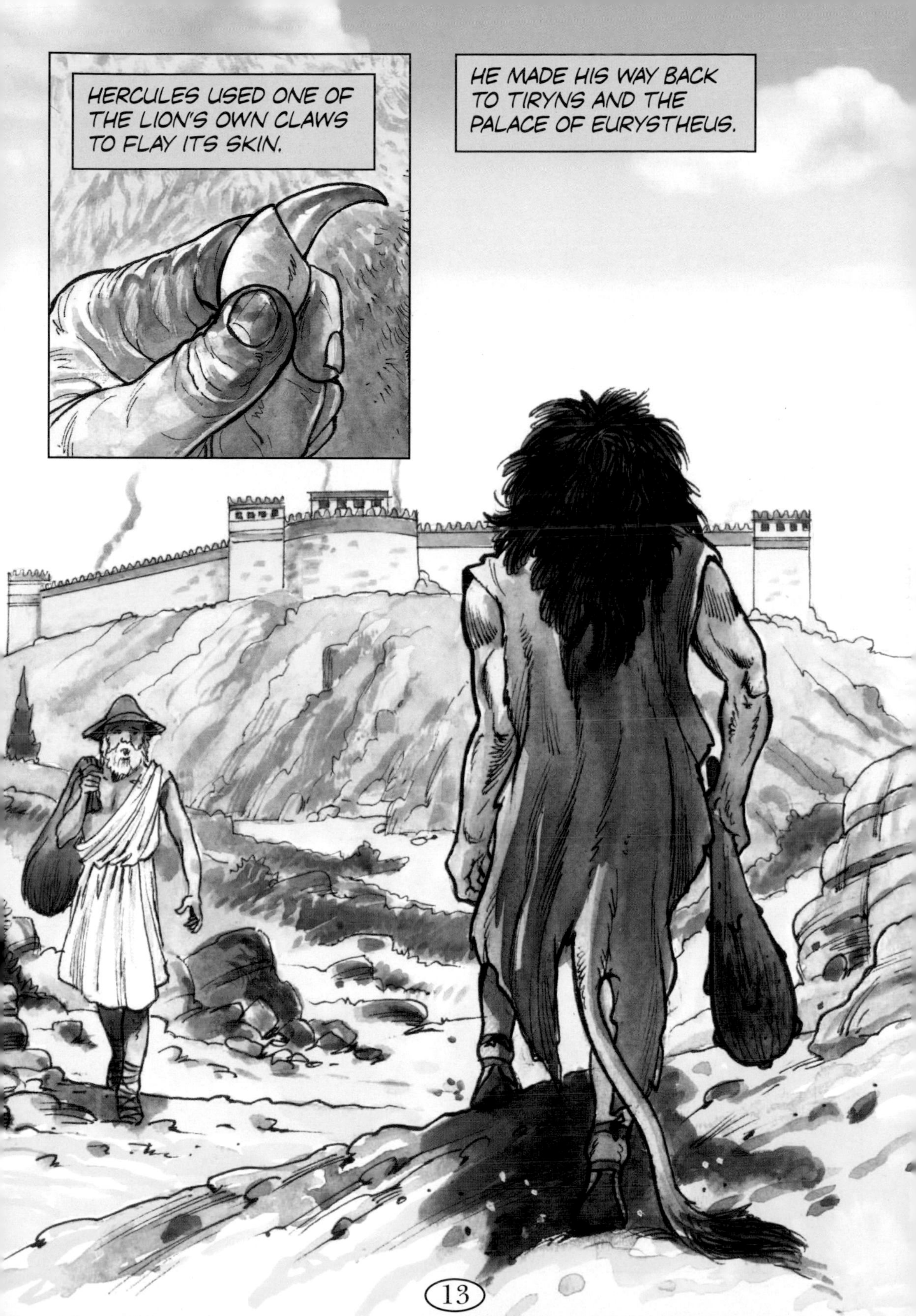
HERCULES USED ONE OF THE LION'S OWN CLAWS TO FLAY ITS SKIN.
HE MADE HIS WAY BACK TO TIRYNS AND THE PALACE OF EURYSTHEUS.

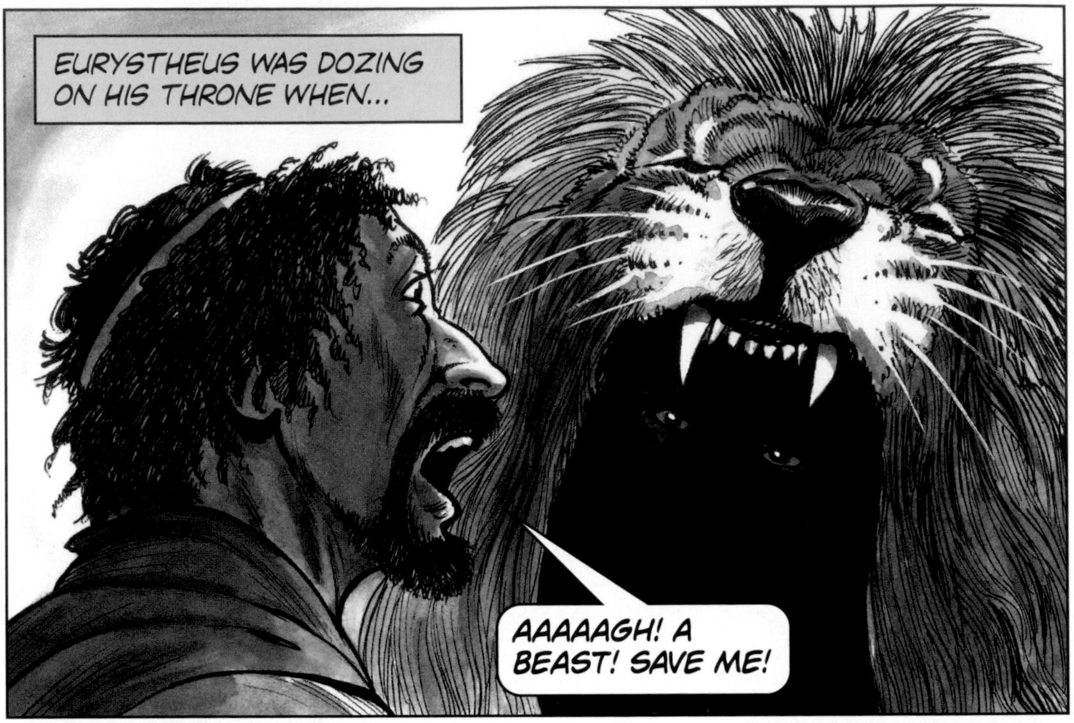
EURYSTHEUS WAS DOZING ON HIS THRONE WHEN...
AAAAAGH! A BEAST! SAVE ME!

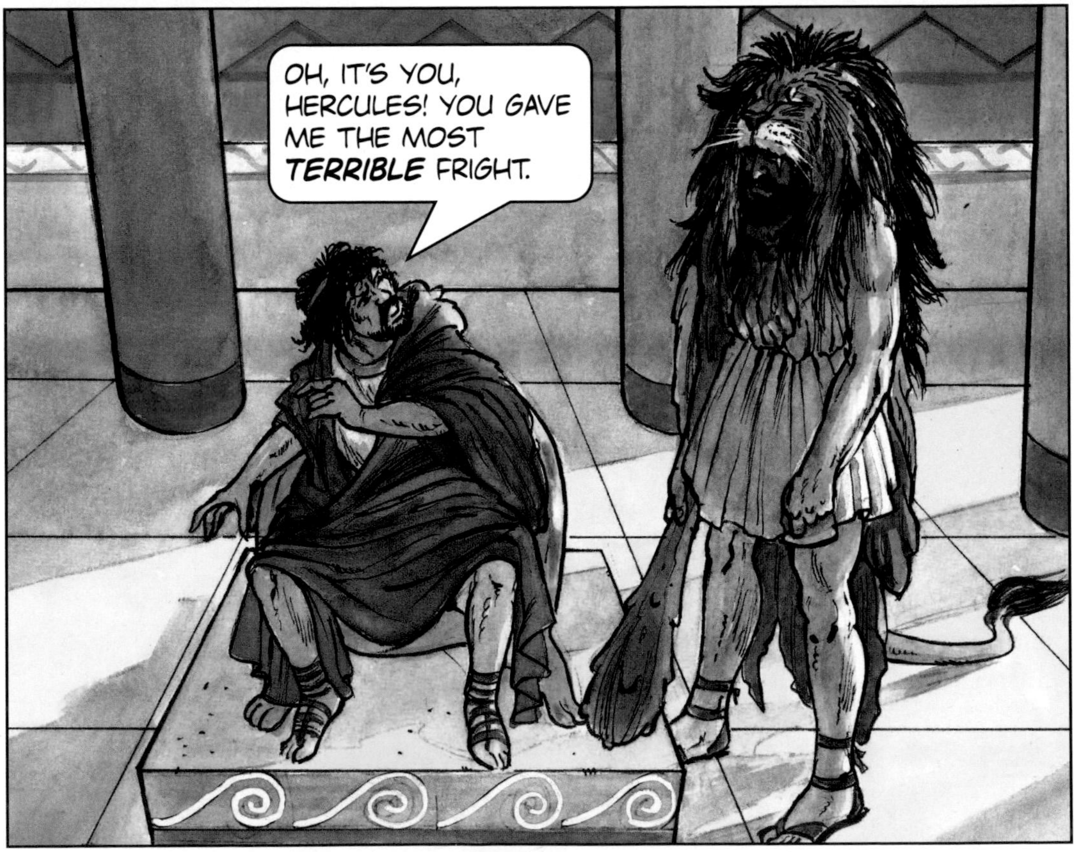
OH, IT'S YOU, HERCULES! YOU GAVE ME THE MOST TERRIBLE FRIGHT.

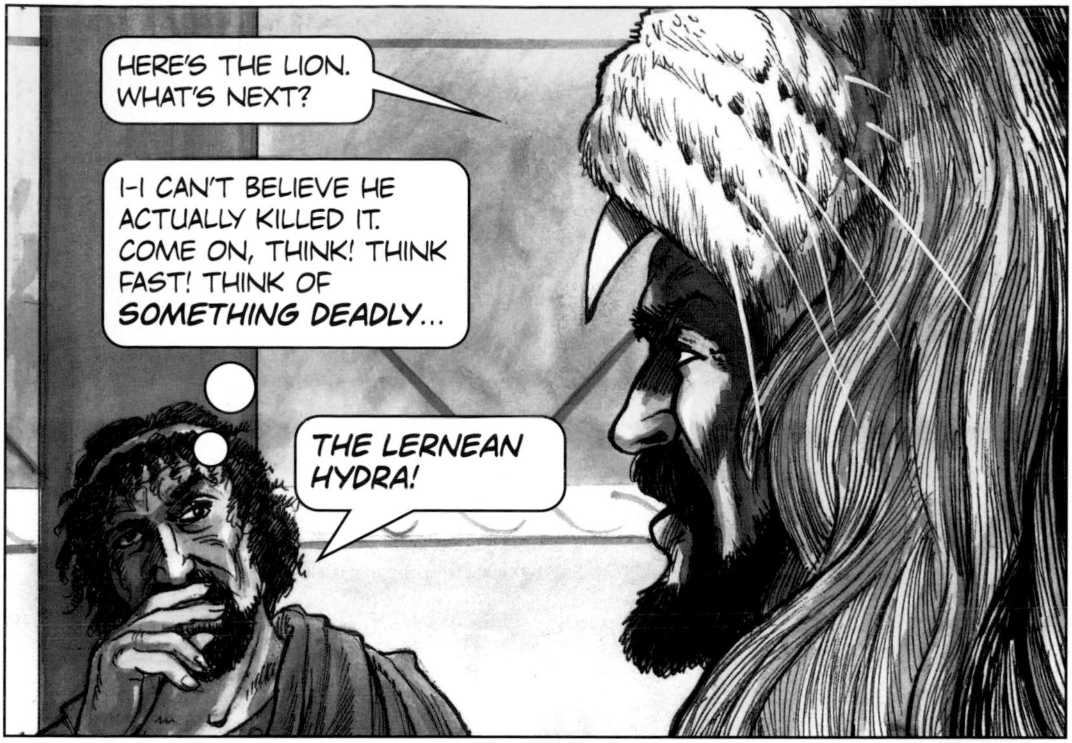
HERE'S THE LION. WHAT'S NEXT?
I-I CAN'T BELIEVE HE ACTUALLY KILLED IT. COME ON, THINK! THINK FAST! THINK OF SOMETHING DEADLY...
THE LERNEAN HYDRA!

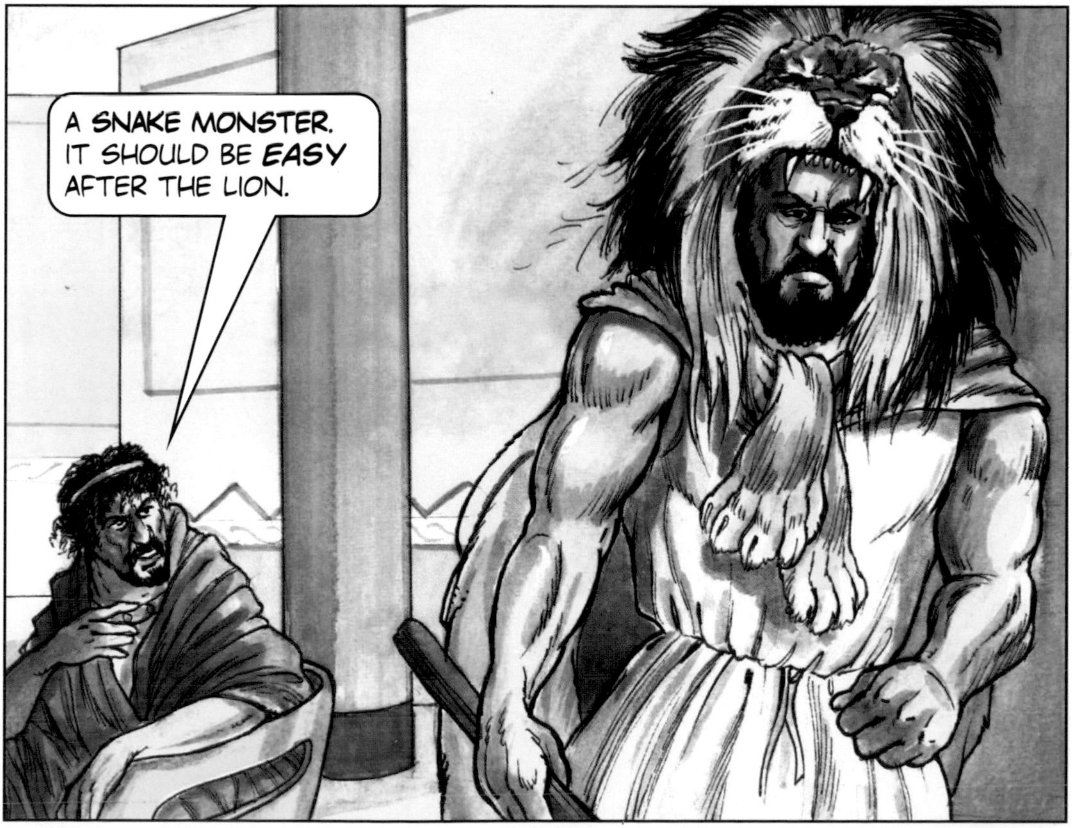
A SNAKE MONSTER. IT SHOULD BE EASY AFTER THE LION.

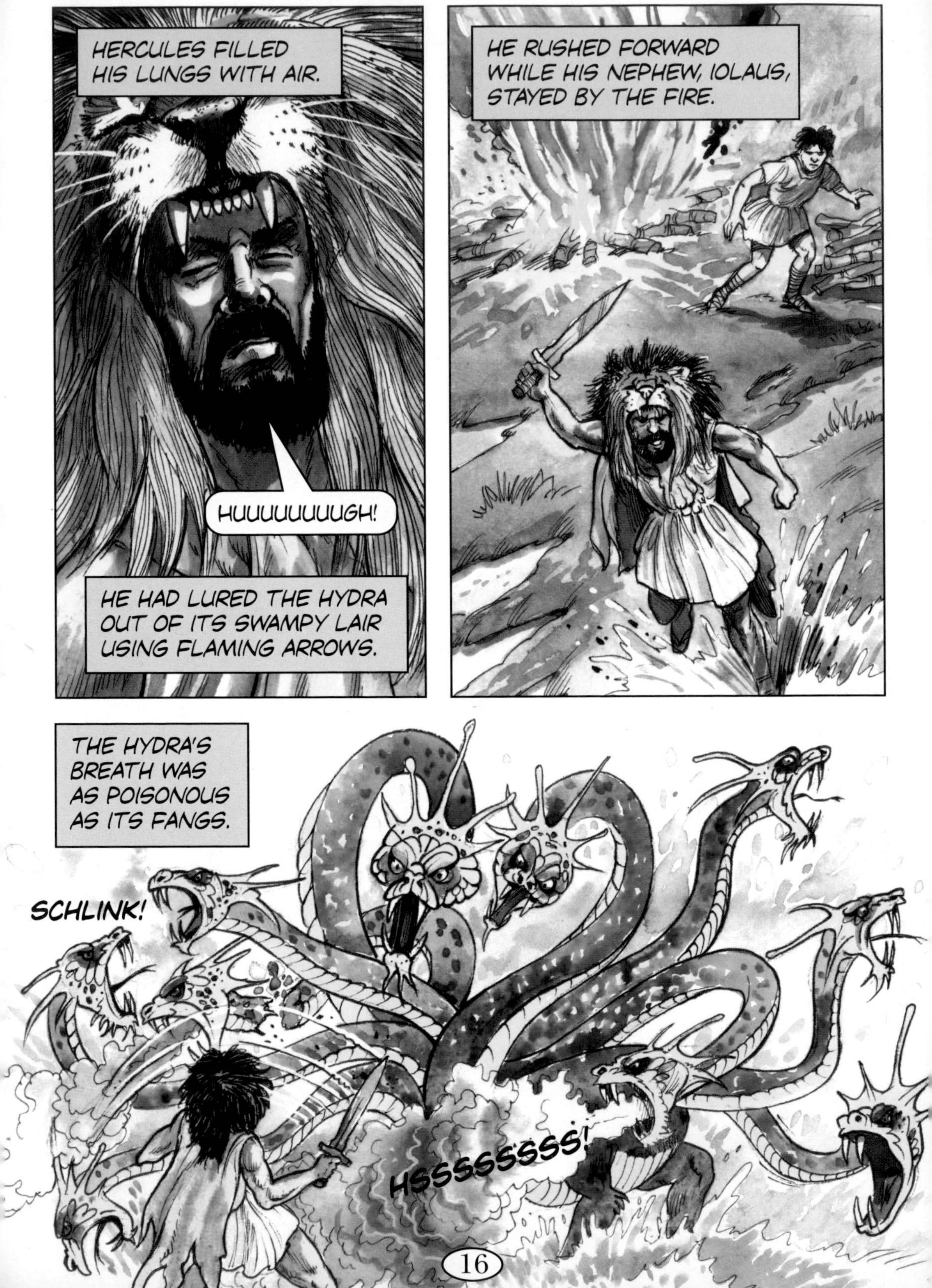
HERCULES FILLED HIS LUNGS WITH AIR.
HUUUUUUUUGH!
HE HAD LURED THE HYDRA OUT OF ITS SWAMPY LAIR USING FLAMING ARROWS.
HE RUSHED FORWARD WHILE HIS NEPHEW, IOLAUS, STAYED BY THE FIRE.
THE HYDRA'S BREATH WAS AS POISONOUS AS ITS FANGS.
SCHLINK!
HSSSSSSSS!

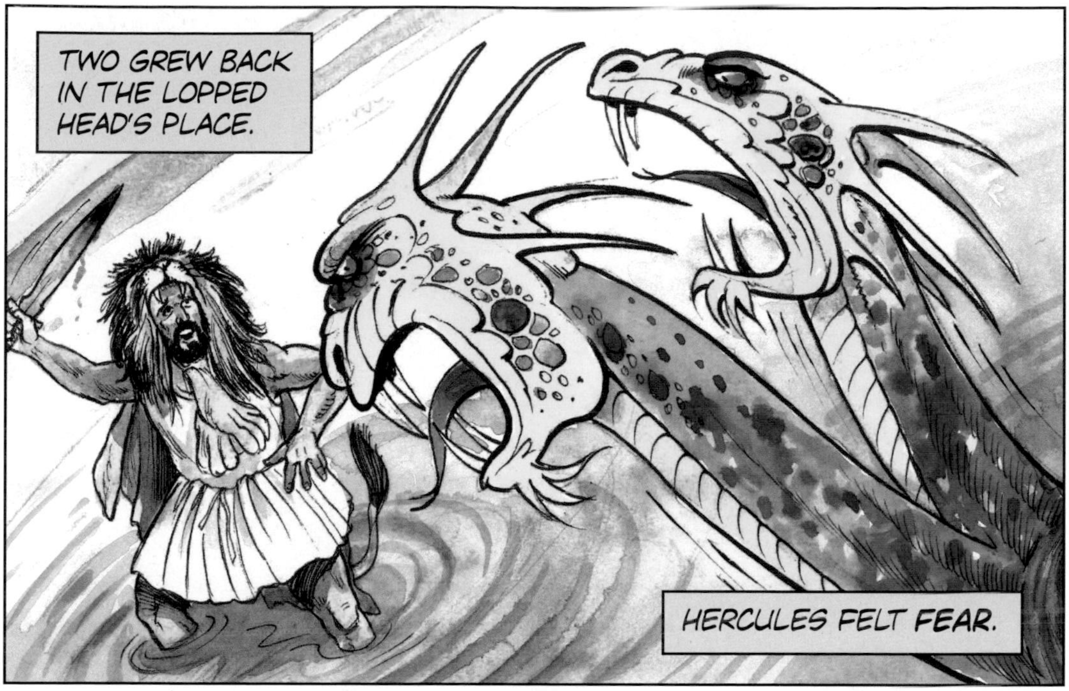
TWO GREW BACK IN THE LOPPED HEAD'S PLACE.
HERCULES FELT FEAR.

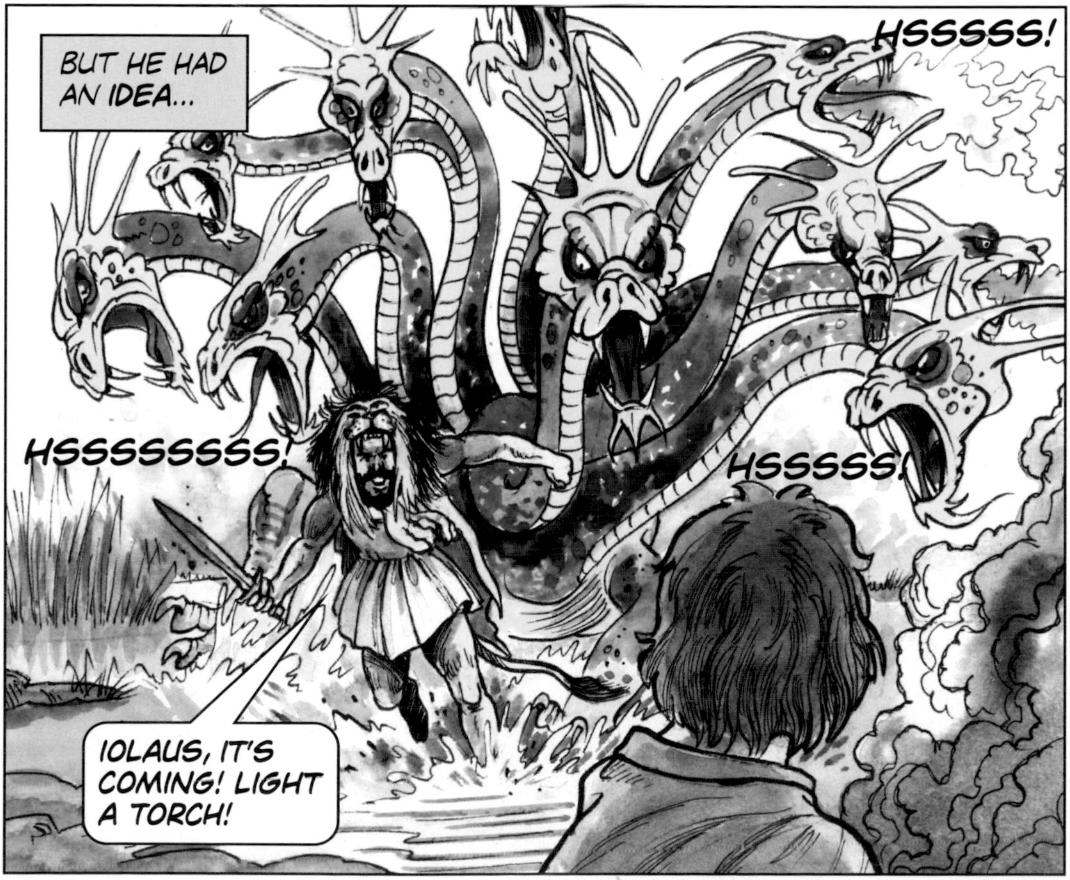
BUT HE HAD AN IDEA...
HSSSSS!
HSSSSSSSS!
HSSSSS!
IOLAUS, IT'S COMING! LIGHT A TORCH!

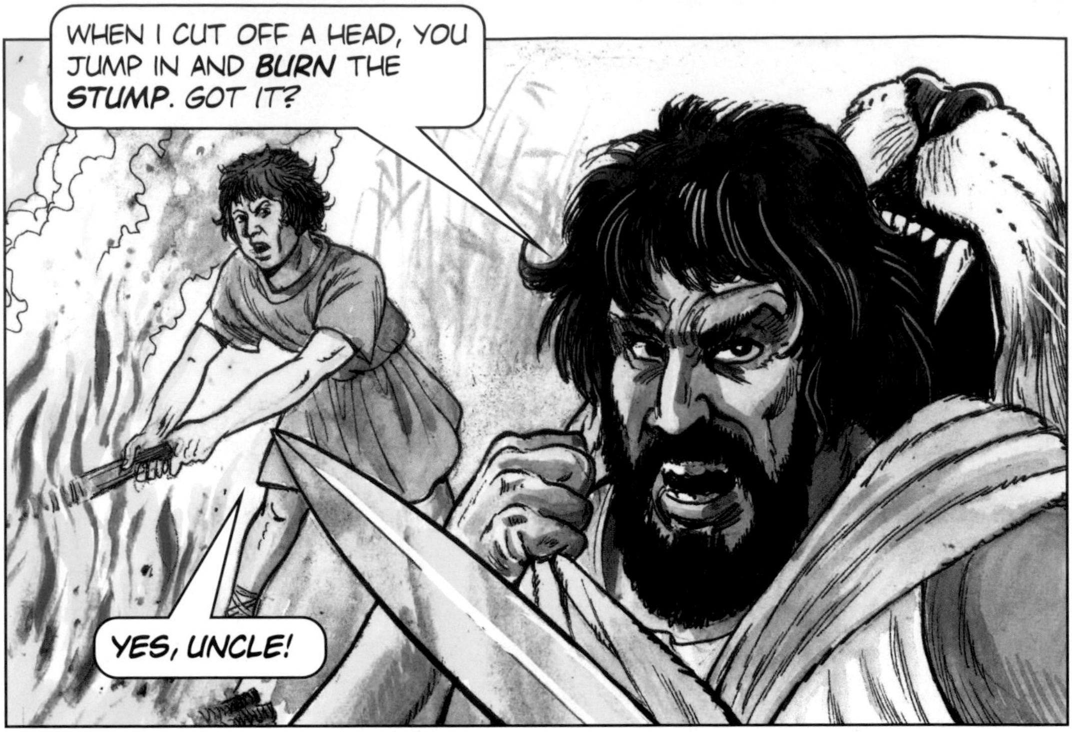
WHEN I CUT OFF A HEAD, YOU JUMP IN AND BURN THE STUMP. GOT IT?
YES, UNCLE!

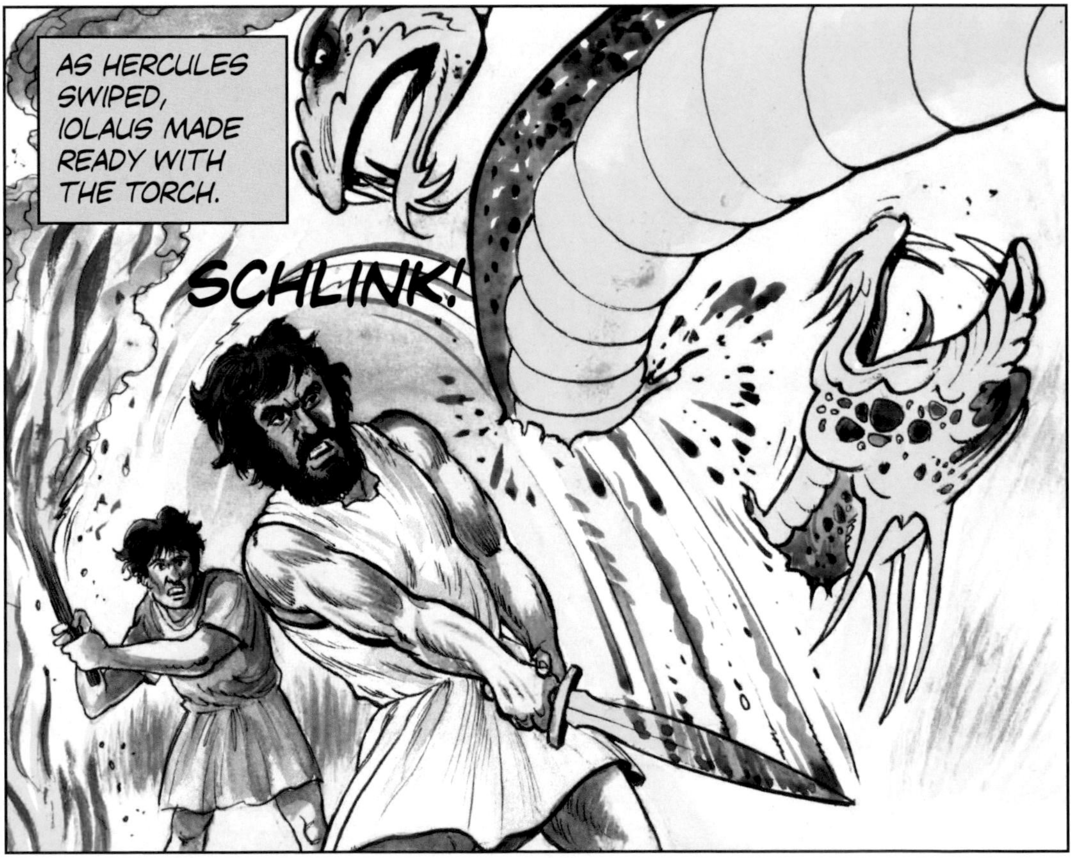
AS HERCULES SWIPED, IOLAUS MADE READY WITH THE TORCH.
SCHLINK!

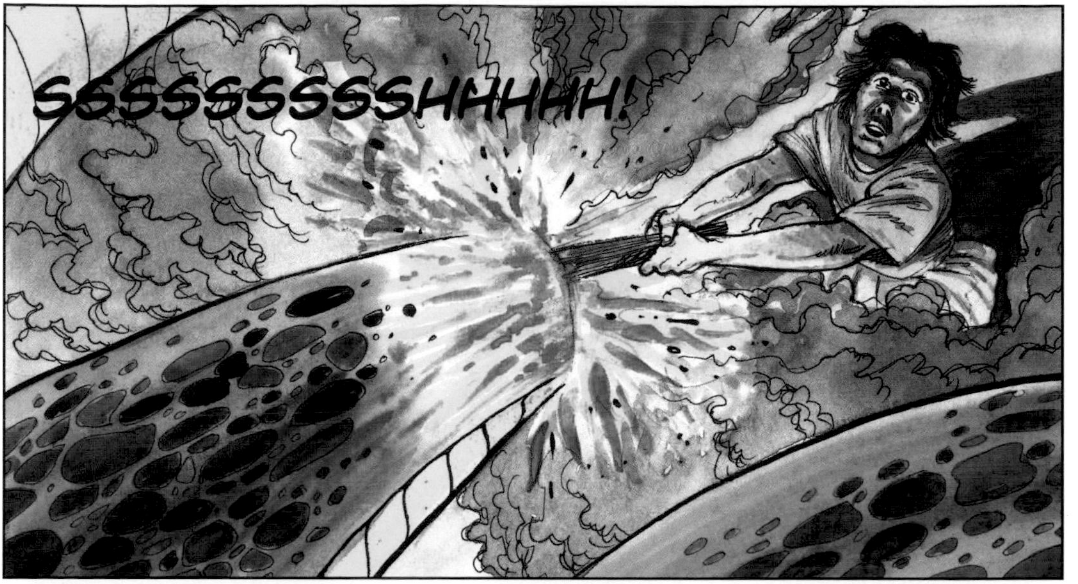
SSSSSSSSSSHHHHH!

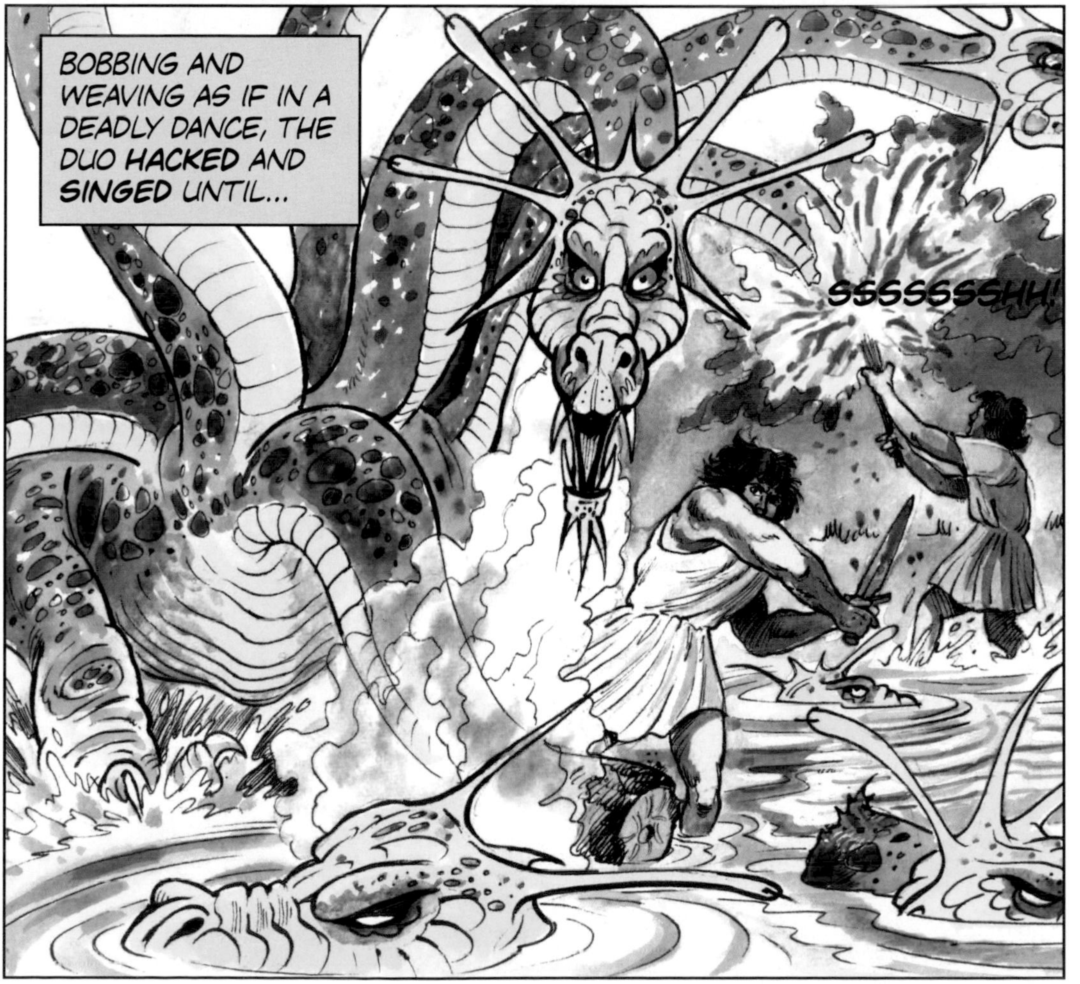
BOBBING AND WEAVING AS IF IN A DEADLY DANCE, THE DUO HACKED AND SINGED UNTIL...
SSSSSSSHH!

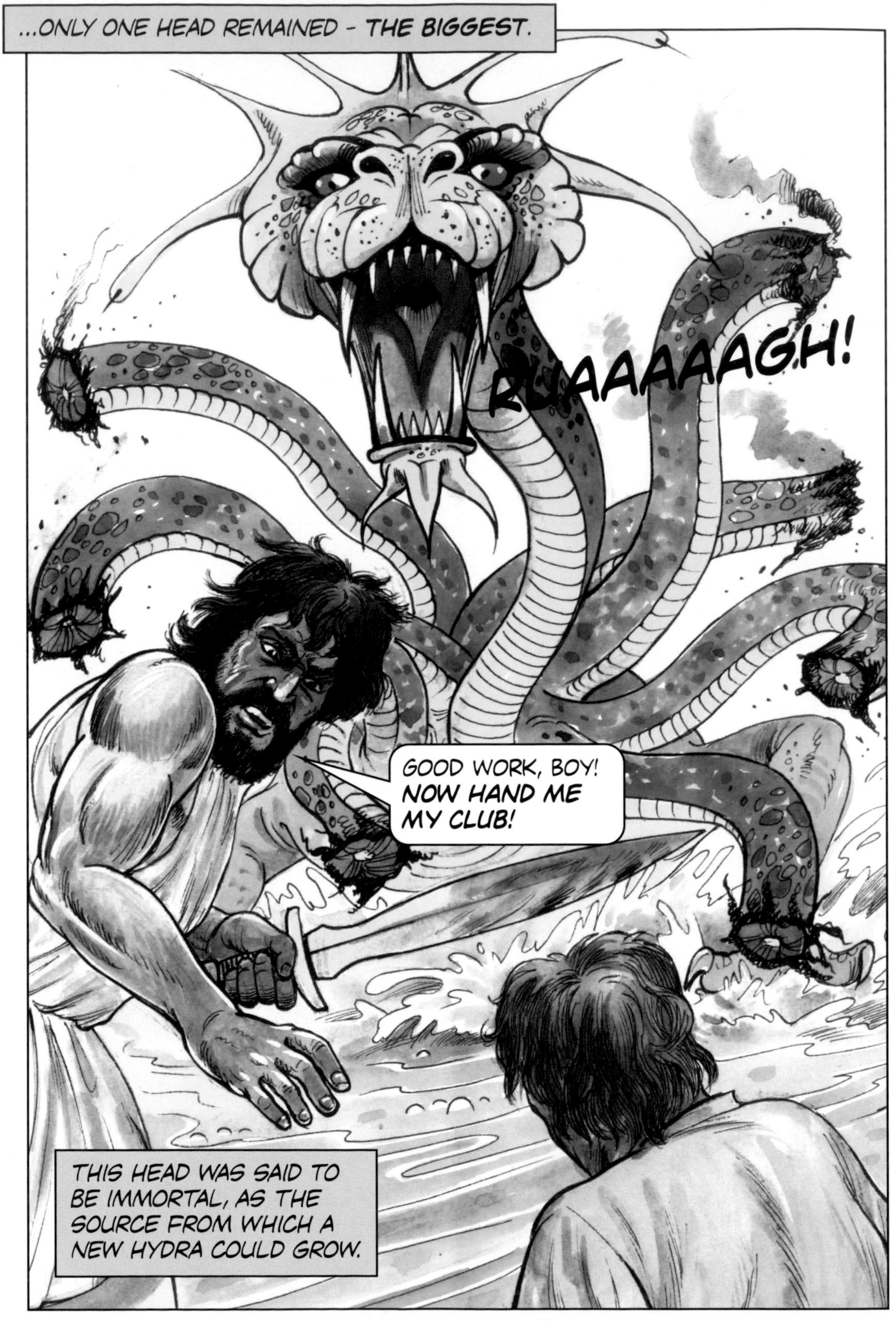
...ONLY ONE HEAD REMAINED - THE BIGGEST.
RUAAAAAAGH!
GOOD WORK, BOY! NOW HAND ME MY CLUB!
THIS HEAD WAS SAID TO BE IMMORTAL, AS THE SOURCE FROM WHICH A NEW HYDRA COULD GROW.

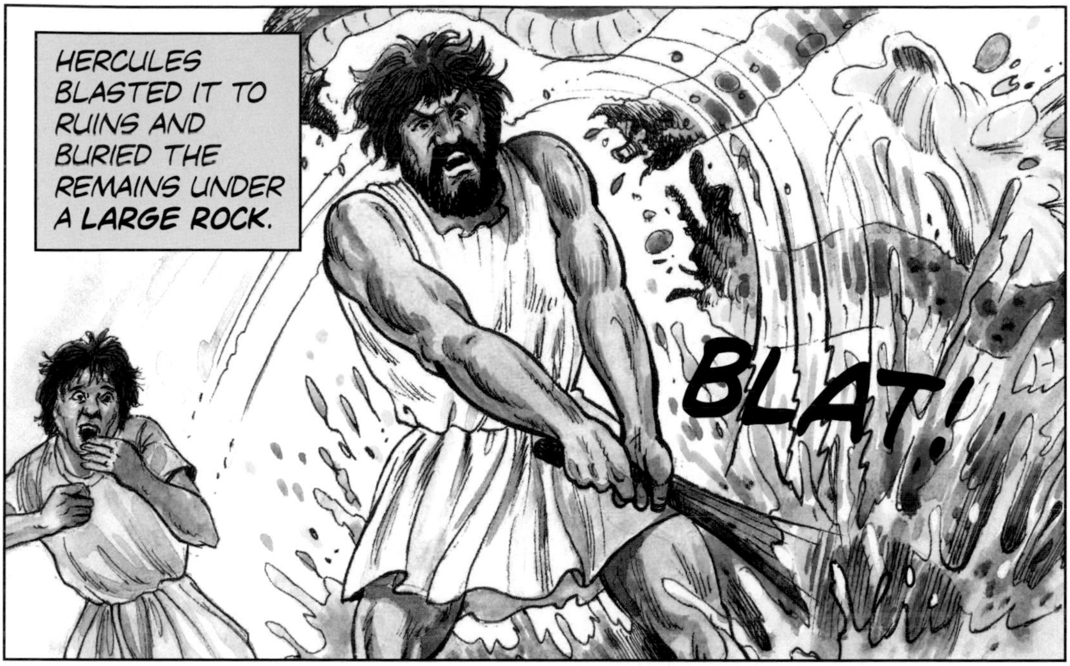
HERCULES BLASTED IT TO RUINS AND BURIED THE REMAINS UNDER A LARGE ROCK.
BLAT!

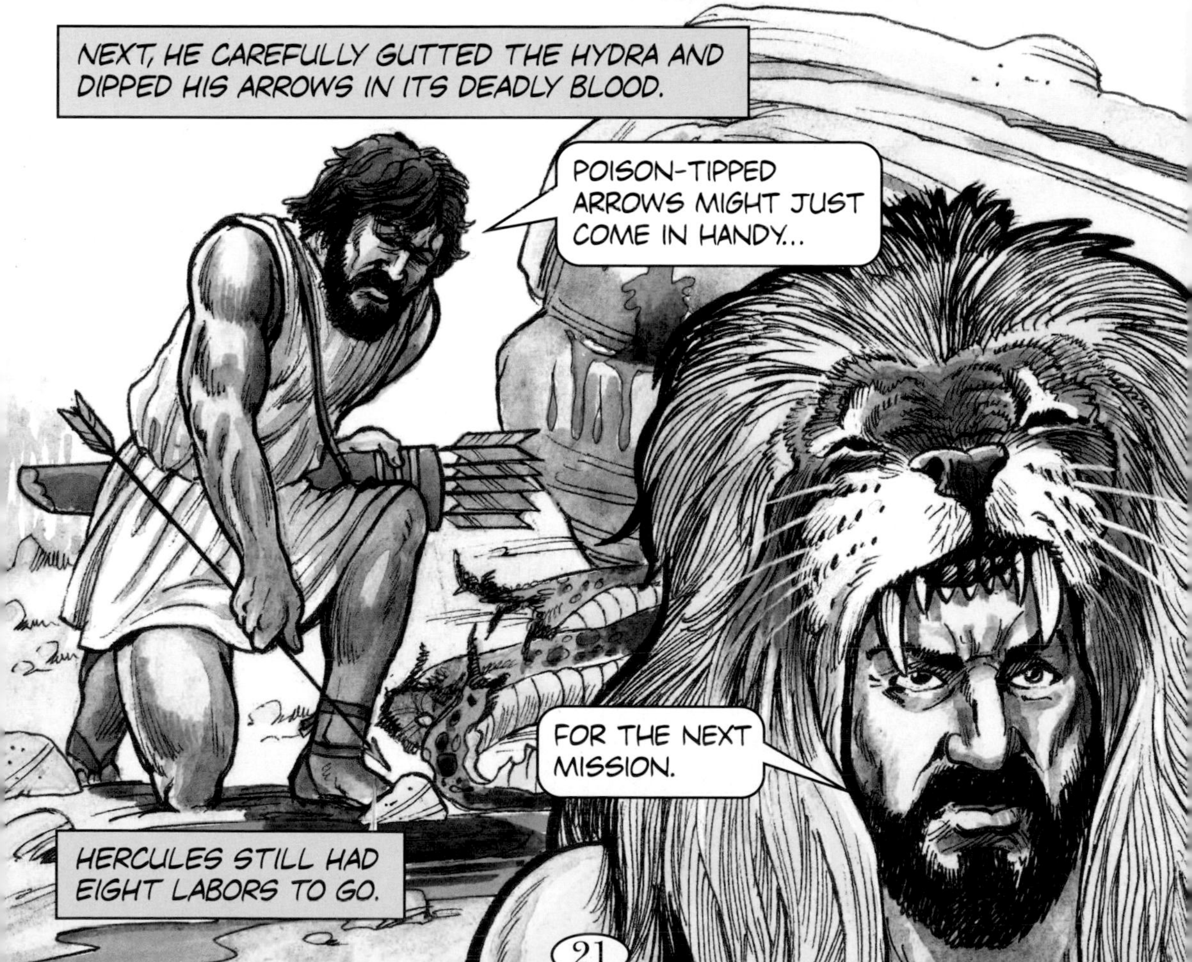
NEXT, HE CAREFULLY GUTTED THE HYDRA AND DIPPED HIS ARROWS IN ITS DEADLY BLOOD.
POISON-TIPPED ARROWS MIGHT JUST COME IN HANDY...
FOR THE NEXT MISSION.
HERCULES STILL HAD EIGHT LABORS TO GO.

When Eurystheus heard about the hydra, he hid in a huge pot in the cellar and sent a herald to give Hercules his next task.

Eight More Labors

Hercules spent a year stalking the **golden hind of Artemis** before successfully capturing the deer alive. Next, he netted the **Erymanthian boar**. The fifth labor was to clean the huge **Augean stables** in a single day, which he did by diverting a river through them. Next, he used a set of magical clangers to scare up and shoot down the enormous flock of **Stymphalian birds**. After all this, capturing the **Cretan bull** proved simple, along with the taming of the flesh-eating **mares of Diomedes**. Unfortunately, Hercules and his men had to battle to gain the famed **girdle of Hippolyta**, queen of the Amazons. Finally, Hercules traveled to the end of the world to claim **Geryon's cattle** by slaying the three-headed, six-legged giant.

"You're Not Finished…"

"…I don't count the hydra—you had help with that. And you arranged to get paid for the Augean stables, so you owe me two more labors," said Eurystheus when Hercules returned.

The second-to-last labor was the stealing of the **apples of the Hesperides**, which Hercules accomplished by tricking Atlas (who held up the heavens) to do it for him. The final labor was trickiest of all—the **taming of Cerberus**, the three-headed dog of the underworld. With these 12 labors completed, Hercules was guaranteed a place with the gods on Mount Olympus when he died.

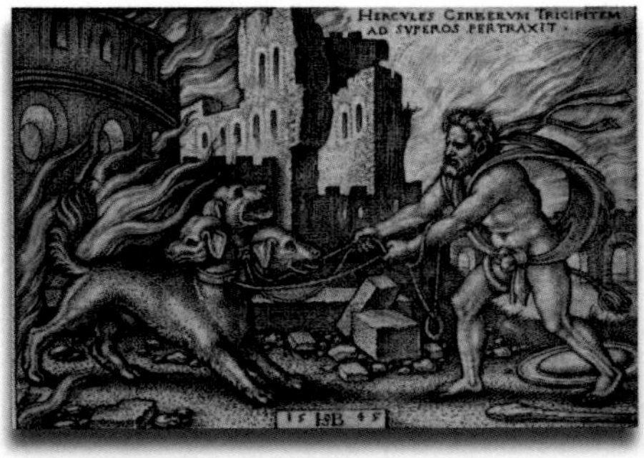
HERCVLES CERBERVM TRICIPITEM
AD SVPEROS PERTRAXIT
Hercules captures Cerberus.

GLOSSARY

battering Hitting repeatedly with a blunt object.

dozing Napping or lightly sleeping.

duo A group of two.

flay To butcher a recently killed animal by cutting it open and removing the skin.

herald A person who delivers messages.

heroic Displaying the courage and skill of a hero.

hydra A snake-like water monster with many heads and poisonous breath and blood.

lair The resting place of a wild animal or a place for hiding.

oracle A wise person who gives advice and makes prophecies.

penance An act that must be completed in order to receive forgiveness for a crime or sin.

prophecy A prediction about the future.

slain Killed.

strangled Violently choked.

INDEX